HEAVEN

"ARE WE THERE YET?"

A Guide to Your Way Back Home

♦

Daryl Chang

Copyright © 2023 Daryl Chang.
All rights reserved. Without prejudice.

This book may not be reproduced in whole or in part in any manner whatsoever without written permission from the author except in the case of brief quotations embodied in critical articles and reviews.

This book is not a form of any fictional man-made legal or medical advice. This book simply serves as fuel for personal inspiration to become wholly conscious of who you truly are. Your actions are always your own self-responsibility.

Front cover image: pixabay.com – Digital Designer
Rear cover image: pixabay.com – Riza April.
Inside images: pixabay.com – Riza April, clker, openclipart, Gordon Johnson.

HEAVEN "ARE WE THERE YET?" A Guide to Your Way Back Home
Daryl Chang
ISBN-13: 978-1-7389410-3-2

Personal Growth, Body Mind & Spirit, Self-help, Spirituality

Also by Daryl Chang
MASQUERADE: The Life Game God Plays
THE MIND OF GOD: Life Behind The Scenes

.

To God who lives within you.
To the Overcomer you are.
Know who *you* are.

Thank you God for all the good things in my life
and for entrusting me to write this book.
Bless the world and *you* who read this book.
All the love, power, and wisdom to you.
God loves you. I love you.

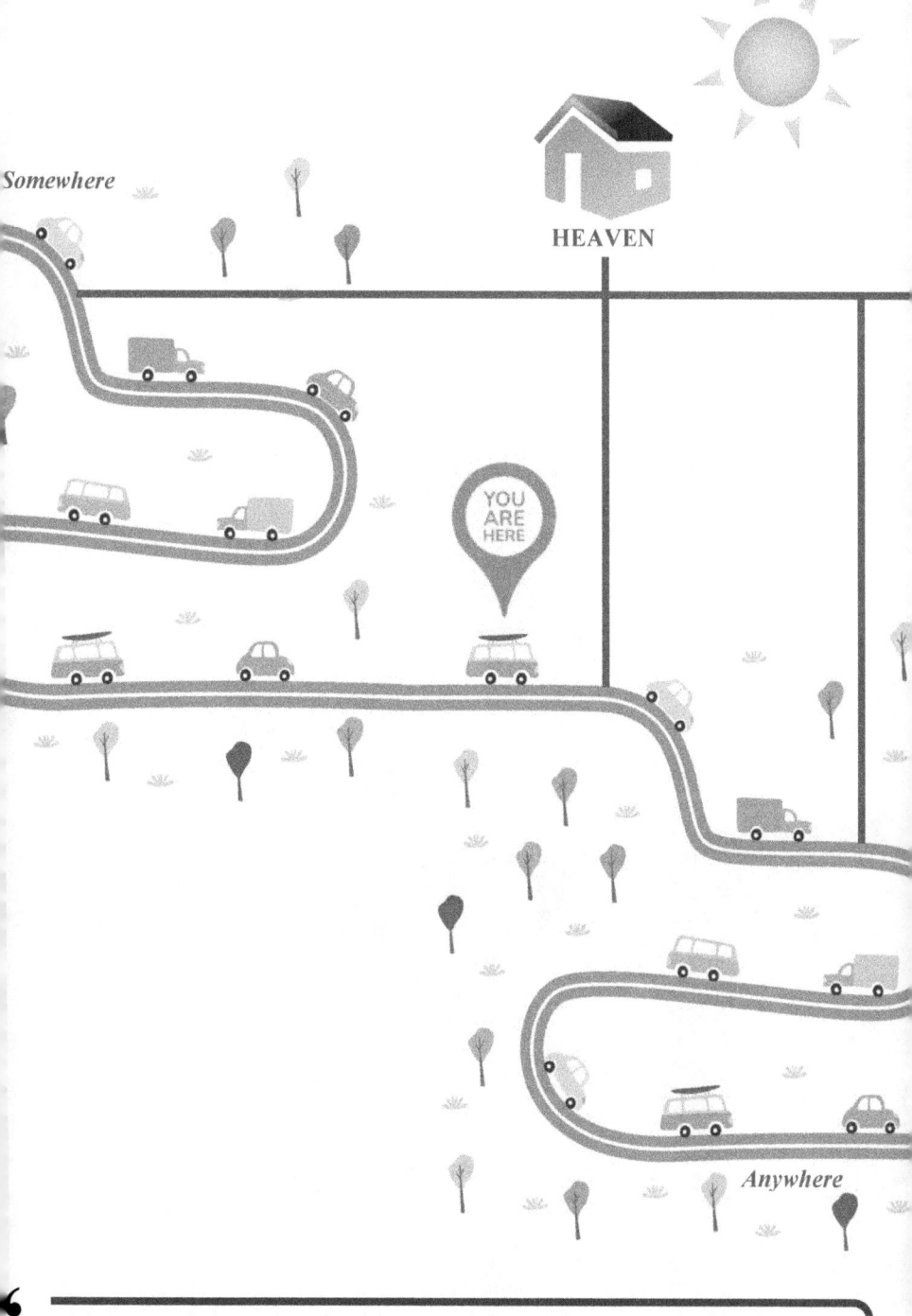

CONTENTS

♦

Preface 1
Prologue 3
Introduction 5

PART ONE - Know Who You Are 9
    CHAPTER 1   The Word God 10
    CHAPTER 2   Motives 12
    CHAPTER 3   Perception 14
    CHAPTER 4   All is God 16
    CHAPTER 5   You Are As God Is 20
    CHAPTER 6   Who You Are Not 22

PART TWO - Claim Your Divinity 23
    CHAPTER 7   Parent & Child 24
    CHAPTER 8   Perfection 27
    CHAPTER 9   Oneness 30
    CHAPTER 10   Spirit 33
    CHAPTER 11   Responsibility 34
    CHAPTER 12   Time 36

PART THREE - Exercise Your Power 37
    CHAPTER 13   Thought 38
    CHAPTER 14   Words 41
    CHAPTER 15   Belief & Faith 45
    CHAPTER 16   Gratitude 47
    CHAPTER 17   Knowing 49
    CHAPTER 18   Blessing 51

PART FOUR - Get There 53
    CHAPTER 19   I AM 54
    CHAPTER 20   Balance 56
    CHAPTER 21   Creation 57
    CHAPTER 22   Acceptance 59
    CHAPTER 23   Love 61

Epilogue 63

Preface

♦

This book points you to a truth which only *you* can believe, determine, experience, know, and accept for yourself.

I offer you thoughts for your consideration. If you are resistant to the thoughts and words you read, I encourage you to ask yourself, "Why am I unwilling to believe the possibility of this truth? Why do I believe this to be untrue and what I presently believe to be true? Is what I currently believe, something I have proved or is it something handed to me by race, superstition, suggestion, or man-made theories?"

All I sincerely ask of you is to be willing to explore and experiment with the ideas, and to earnestly try applying the principles to see what results. Prove it to yourself. The ease and progress of doing so is based on how deep the level is of your willingness.

Prologue
♦

Many think that there are lots of problems in this world but in actuality, there is only one problem. For certain, there are multiple problems displayed as war, poverty, dis-ease, tyranny, oppression, pollution, et cetera. But all derive from the one problem – your separation from God. To say it another way, you are disconnected from your Source – *God*. You do not know about your own divine nature and its relation to the universe. More simply, you do not *truly* know who you are.

You may be inclined to quickly dismiss the simplicity of this declaration and put the book down. I encourage you to be open to it if you want to sincerely contribute to a joyous world and to your own joyous life.

Why is this important to me but ultimately you? When you are unaware of your divinity and your power, you are easily deceived, manipulated, and intimidated, and you submit to the creative power and energy of people around you. The less you claim of the power you have to create your life, the more others create it for you. The result is the apparent problems of the world you find yourself in.

All problems arise from fear. They are all physical manifestations or reflections of fear. This is another or equivalent way of stating the aforementioned one problem – the only problem to solve is one of fear.

Trying to solve one problem is a less daunting task than trying to solve thousands. Fortunately, the one solution to the one problem is the same for all problems. Both the problem and solution lies within you; your mind. The problem is simple – *you do not know who you are*; the solution is simple – *know who you are*. This is to say, you are the problem and you are the solution. The solution answers all questions and collapses all problems. Would you like to better understand the problem and the solution to what seems like a world of complexities? "Yes," I can hear you say. Hence, I have written this book for you. Read on.

Introduction

"The journey of a thousand miles begins with one step."
~ Lao Tzu ~

♦

Heaven is your original home; your real home.

This place you currently live and settle in permanently for your daily life; a life filled with much challenge, negativity, and suffering; a life you have accepted as normal existence – *this world is not your home*. It has made you regularly long for a vacation destination that allows you to escape temporarily this everyday life. In fact, much of the activities you do nowadays (ie. movies, music, alcohol, drugs, et cetera) whether for social, entertainment, or amusement purposes as you perceive, is really a means to escape pain, thought, or the life you deem normal.

The life you have been led to live is reversed from truth. That is, the vacation destination you dream of where you are free and experience joy, peace, happiness, and all things good is rightly your permanent residence; whilst the life you presently deem normal is temporary when you inadvertently slip and then remember who you are.

You do not take the time to ask questions and contemplate the falsity of your current existence. You are kept intentionally busy, distracted, and overwhelmed by false authorities to ensure that you do not so that you remain as you are (ie. a slave).

You innately know that you do not enjoy seeing or experiencing suffering of any kind (ie. war, poverty, famine, oppression, hatred, et cetera) and yet it persists unceasingly. You know something isn't right but you cannot put your finger on it. At a deep level, you want better but you feel powerless to affect positive change on a global scale, yet alone your own individual circumstances.

You do not think so but you are your own worst enemy because your mind is closed. You impede the personal growth and development of yourself particularly when you have had a negative experience. Though you may have goals, you unwittingly sabotage yourself from advancing and achieving your goals by no longer being open to what you have closed.

Let's say you decide you want to go somewhere to experience joy, peace, happiness, fun, and all things good. You need to know where you are going and you need to know how to get there. So before you head out on your road trip, you review a map on how to get there and pack all the necessary and useful stuff you need.

Your life's journey is no different in principle. If you determine your dream destination is Heaven – where only love and light abide –, then you need an up-to-date map that shows you the path there while making the adventure an enjoyable experience. I offer you information as a map to this end. As you embark on your journey henceforth (of self-discovery), may your experience be filled with joy, peace, and love because of it. In order to effectively convey the book's message, the book is organized into four sections.

Part One, "Know Who You Are," offers a framework to have you recognize personal obstacles and motives, the essence of your being, and your relation to the universe – so that you advance to knowing who you are.

Part Two, "Claim Your Divinity," takes the background from Part One to establish context you use to claim your divinity now that you are aware of who you are.

Part Three, "Exercise Your Power," unites the content from Part One and Part Two and explains the tools you use to exercise your innate power of love.

Part Four, "Get There," consolidates the knowledge of the prior sections and provides practical advice to reach the intended destination.

Throughout it all, you will need to bring courage, open-mindedness, humility, and a deep willingness to enjoy, apply, and assimilate what I share with you in these pages.

To reach your destination, there is actually nothing to do but change the concept of yourself and that is accomplished by simply knowing who you are.

I will tell you now that the information here is not actually anything new per se. Sages, philosophers, and others – Jesus being the most notable – have known this great "secret" truth and have tried to convey it to all. Alas, the truth has been grasped by relatively few people. I write this book in my own personal expression to help you understand this truth. I have merely organized and delivered my thoughts, which are your thoughts, to help you gain clarity.

The reason you do not practically know what you innately know but have forgotten is because you have been busy doing more than merely being who you are. If you reverse your behaviour such that you focus on being who you are, your doing will follow naturally. You do not know this because you do not take the time to remove yourself from the noise of this world and be still.

At present moment, this may not make any sense. As you continue to read the information within these pages, you may possibly say that nothing I express is ingenious or enlightening yet you will become enlightened. Your awakening will have begun and you will begin the path to creating a joyous world and a joyous life. This is my wish for you, me, and all mankind.

PART ONE
Know Who You Are

The Essence of Your Being

CHAPTER 1
The Word God

"A closed mind is like a window shut because of the winter cold, never to be opened again for fresh air, not knowing that the season changes."

♦

Recognize that all words exist because its origin is from Oneness. Do not overly concern yourself at present moment if you are unfamiliar with this term. This is particularly evident with words that express dualities or polarities (ie. deemed opposites); they are on the same continuum. The key to everything in life is a complete understanding and appreciation of Oneness: *God.*

No matter what your belief is, undeniably, there is a "source" of creation. This "source" has been given many names such as God, Source, Creator, Divine, the Power, Higher Intelligence, Creative Principle, and Universal Consciousness. Whichever word you are comfortable with, it is simply the attempt to label that creative "source" of existence which goes beyond our human intellectual comprehension. I use the word God as the Source of creation because it is short and sweet, and I am comfortable with it.

Churches and religion have intentionally distorted the image of God to control people and nations. They have successfully defamed God to create numerous factions. They have fashioned atheists to not believe in God; agnostics to not know what to believe of God; and firm believers to believe in God outside of themselves and a God of their making. They have mixed lies and truths to create confusion and misunderstanding of God. They have shaped copious religions across the globe to compete and fight amongst themselves as to whose God is the true God. They have implemented endless propaganda to this date so that many no longer suspect their deception and elaborate schemes.

Many of this world especially individuals who apparently have had dreadful experiences brought up in religious families, are completely turned off by the mere mention of the word God. They view God with absolute disdain. As such, they have closed their mind to God. While understandable, this is unfortunate because they reject any discussion of the true God, thereby impeding their own soul advancement.

If you are such an individual, you need to be willing to overcome your aversion to this word. You must temporarily suspend your judgment, beliefs, and feelings. You must be open to the possibility that what you have been manipulated to believe is untrue. If the meaning or premise of your beliefs is not true, then how you have been operating and still are will in turn be false. Hence, you sustain your continued suffering and hinder progress, not only of yourself but of the collective world.

The sequence of information in the book is purposeful. Each part builds on that which precedes it and is integral to the overall process of self-realization. If you feel resistance to reading further, that is okay but let it not stop you from continuing. Continue to read and try not to judge what you read as you read it. Instead, read with your heart and feel what the words mean to you rather than trying to understand them rationally. Much will resonate with you immediately and much will need to be kept on the back burner of your mind until it makes sense. Little by little you may notice that your resistance dwindles.

CHAPTER 2
Motives

"To the mind that is still, the whole universe surrenders."
~ Lao Tzu ~

♦

In every moment, you are changing and evolving in an attempt to stay in balance. Your intent is to have balance in your state of mind and your physical experience. This balance comes from a sense of satisfaction, joy, and peace from what you experience and how you define yourself. When you do not feel fulfilled about your experiences and who you are, you explore ways to restore balance.

Your life is a journey. You cultivate your life according to your level of awareness and your beliefs. These two main factors determine how you see and define yourself, which in turn determine your life experiences.

With limited consciousness, some beliefs, for example, that are limiting to your personal growth and life are: you are a victim of circumstances and have no control over your life; you have to work hard to attain success; you are not destined for greatness; your life has no meaning and purpose; you lack skill or talent; you do not have enough money to do what you want; you are not good enough; you are not loved.

If you identify with any of the aforementioned beliefs, you may find it hard to accept the idea that it is *you* who created your conditions. You will not believe, understand, or accept that the fault is yours alone and that you created your unhappiness. Why and how would *you* personally create what *you* know is not what *you* want?

You are always seeking balance, the state of mind of clarity, peace, and contentment. This sense of balance is achieved faster and will remain with you longer through an expansion of awareness that reveals more of who you really are.

The most crucial realization of your life is that *you* alone control it and that *you* create your own experience of it. When you finally discover that you are in control and that you create it all, you will have a sense of relief and joy because this means you have the power to change it all and create instead the experiences that make you joyful, peaceful, and successful. This comes about when you finally discover your divinity and who you truly are.

CHAPTER 3
Perception

"Wisdom is found only in truth."
~ Johann Wolfgang von Goethe ~
♦

Everything you experience is according to your perception. Everything is considered either a reality or an illusion. The way you perceive your reality depends upon what you believe is true. How do you know if your perception is true of what you deem reality?

In its simplest form, you think reality is that which exists in actuality, that which is "real"; while illusion is that which does not exist, that which is "unreal". At present moment, you habitually determine what is real or illusory by your physical senses.

An illusion is that which you perceive existing in such a way as to cause misinterpretation of its actual nature. Illusion is that which is ever changing. Conversely, reality is that which does not change.

If you understand the aforementioned, then you will concede that what you see and experience in this physical world is perpetually changing, hence an illusion. In contrast, God which is all in all is unwavering, immutable, and beneficent, thus reality – the only reality. Whatever God is *is* reality; whatever God is not *is* illusion.

Your perception of what you now deem reality is a misinterpretation of the actual nature of God, of yourself.

Everything that you see and experience in this physical world with your physical senses is an illusion created by you to experience your thoughts and consciousness first hand. When you have wrong thoughts, you experience negative circumstances, predicaments, or forms of suffering so as to guide you back to God. The illusion or apparent reality is for your benefit so that you may correct them.

The error in your perception of reality occurs because you do not know who you are; because your current beliefs are unfounded. You must know that truth – *God* – never varies. If you believe in not-good (ie. evil, poverty, dis-ease, et cetera) then the not-good will appear. But the not-good is wholly non-existent; it has reality only because you believe in it. It is illusion. If you no longer have the belief which gives you the reality it possesses, then it ceases to have the appearance of reality. From the instant that your belief ceases, you recognize that you are free from the condition produced by it.

If you continue to have an illusion of who you are, you will only create bigger illusions of yourself and of the world. The illusion can only be dissolved by seeing the truth.

God persistently personifies that which is. Thus, when you turn from the recognition of the not-good and lack to the recognition of good and supply, and you claim the good, the good will reveal itself to you. This then is reality, the only reality.

CHAPTER 4
All is God

*"You are an infinite expression of love
who has been created from an infinite source of love."*

♦

Take time to contemplate.

Put a seed into the soil. In a relatively short time, it sprouts, breaks the surface, and grows. Ask yourself, "How does it do this?" Did it go to a plant school during the time it was underground to earn a degree to learn how to do this? Really, how does it know how to do this? There must be a higher power, a higher intelligence that is doing this.

Observe a bird flying in the sky. Ask yourself, "How does it do this?" Does it go to some bird aviation school to earn a degree to learn how to do this? Really, how does it know how to do this? There must be a higher power, a higher intelligence that is doing this.

Contemplate anything in nature and ask the same question. You will end up with the same answer.

Reflect on a mother having a baby. At no time does the mother personally provide instructions to the things inside her body to do this and do that to grow the baby. The baby just develops. Just like the seed, ask yourself, "How does it do this?" There is a higher power, a higher intelligence that is doing this.

Now, turn to yourself. Contemplate on your breathing. Do you "do" 'breathing'? That is, do you personally instruct yourself, your body, on how to go about breathing? You do not. It just happens. Do you "do" 'circulating blood'? Do you personally instruct your body on how to circulate your blood and distribute the oxygen throughout? You do not. It just happens. Do you "do" 'digesting food'? Do you personally instruct your body and coordinate all your organs to digest your food? You do not. It just happens. So if you are not doing the breathing, the blood circulating, and the food digesting, then who is doing it? I will give you a clue. It is not Peter, Paul, or Mary. Did you answer the question yourself? It is the higher power, the higher intelligence. It is God. God is in you, just as It is in me, the seed, the flower, the tree, the bird, the squirrel, the sun, the moon, the air, and so on and so on. It is in everything. God is in all and God is all.

God is behind the mask and costume that every human being wears: the good person, the bad person, the ugly person, the beautiful person, the cripple, the vagrant, the drug addict, the tyrant, et cetera.

Man is the physical form of expression of God in Its likeness.

God works through you like It does through every seed, every bird, every human being, every creature, and so on. God is always working for your good and toward your good. God, the Infinite Intelligence, is always guiding you and revealing to you the answer or solution to your problem. You must accept the truth that the nature of Infinite Intelligence is to respond to you. Your world is your consciousness objectified. The awareness of this truth is the key to every door in life.

If you are like the seed and simply allow God to work through you unimpeded and do what It does, then all things are taken care of. You would purposely blossom into the ultimate unique expression you are as does the flower from the seed.

You are a unique expression of God as every man is and as every creature is. You are just one individual expression of all expressions. Unlike other creatures though, you are in Its image and likeness.

So, there is not man and God. There is not even animal, plant, and man. There is only One Source; only One Creative Power; only One Life; only One Consciousness; only One Mind. There is only One – *God*.

You and God are one. More simply, God is you and you are God. This is a fact. This is knowledge, wisdom, and power. This is truth. *This is who you are.*

The aforementioned is a profound declaration and quite a revelation. Oftentimes, something simple yet unfathomable is not so easy to accept as true. But this is just a habit from your limited (intellectual) thinking because you are not conscious of who you are yet. This is the irony of your current predicament – a predicament that is the foundation to the apparent problems and solution of this world.

It is not arrogance to think you are God when you are. It is ignorance to think you are not when you are. It is through ignorance that you allow the arrogance of others to take your power to use as their own for selfish purposes. It is through ignorance that you misuse your power and then blame others for negative circumstances which result. It is through ignorance that you condemn yourself to unnecessary suffering.

If you have remained open at this point, then this truth is now a seed in your consciousness. If you nurture this seed by providing it with proper soil, water, and sun, then the truth of yourself will be revealed in time and you will live up to your full potential. The question right now is, "Are you willing to nurture this seed to an expanded awareness of who you are and what is possible for you in life, one that is filled with joy?"

When you fully recognize, believe, know, and accept this truth of who you are, it sets you "free" from the unconsciousness of your being (ie. your existence).

To begin unlocking the potential of who you are, you must first understand what this means. That is, who or what is God? What are the characteristics or attributes of God?

God is the Source of creation.

God is omnipotent, omniscient, and omnipresent. That is, It is all-powerful, all-knowing, and all-around.

God is the formless invisible animating intelligent force of energy – *Spirit* – that penetrates, permeates, and fills the spaces and interspaces of the universe of which it is Itself. God is also the visible forms produced from its invisible Self. God is the sum of all things visible and invisible. God is all in all. God is Oneness.

God is eternal and infinite. God has no beginning and no ending. God is the circle of existence. God is perpetually expanding. God is your supply and It is infinite or inexhaustible.

God is consciousness. It is the Universal Mind, the One Mind. It is the Supreme or Infinite Intelligence.

God is absolute, whole, complete, and perfect.

God is wholly love, purity, light, joy, peace, harmony, happiness, compassion, kindness, abundance, calmness, stillness, inclusion, beauty, freedom, non-judgment, non-attachment, non-resistance, health, youth, clarity, knowledge, wisdom, and all things good.

God is wholly perfect good. God is merely a different way of spelling good. Contained within the word good is God and contained within the God in you is good.

God is truth. God is reality.

CHAPTER 5
You Are As God Is

"There are far better things ahead than the ones we leave behind."
~ C.S. Lewis ~

♦

You are one with God. You are made in Its image and likeness. As such, know and accept that whatever God is, you are.

Let's review the statements I have made about God.

God is the Source of creation. Hence, you are the source of your creations. You are the creator, the creation process, and the creation itself. You are the movie maker, the leading actor in your movie, and the movie itself. You are the sculptor, the clay, and the sculpture itself. You are the artist, the paints, and the painting itself. You are the baker, the ingredients and recipe, and the cake itself. You are the law maker, the law process, and the law itself. You are the giver, the giving, and the gift itself. You are all in all.

God is omnipotent, omniscient, and omnipresent. Hence, you are all-powerful, all-knowing, and all-around. You are power and your own master. No one should ever wield power over you. You know the answer to all questions and all problems. You are all in all.

God is absolute. Hence, you are absolute. The absolute cannot contain something within itself that is not itself. As there is no other, you must command yourself to be that which you claim to be or have. You dwell within every conception of yourself and from this inwardness; you transcend all conceptions of yourself only as you believe yourself to be that which you transcend.

God is whole and complete. Hence, you are whole and complete. You do not require anything or anyone to make you whole or complete as you already are.

God is spirit. God is eternal and infinite. Hence, you are spirit, and you are eternal and infinite. You do not fear death because there is no such thing. Death of the physical body is merely one experience of your spiritual awareness in its current existence. Otherwise, there is no end to how you decide to express yourself.

God is consciousness. Hence, you are this consciousness. You are aware of your consciousness. This very awareness of being *is* God, the only God.

God is the Universal Mind, the One Mind. Hence, you are the One Mind connected to all other minds of the One Mind.

God is love. God is good. Hence, you are love and you are good. All that is not love and not good (ie. fear and its derivatives) is not you but serve as signposts to return you to You – *God*.

What you are, that only you can see. As such, the kingdom of God – *Heaven* – is within you.

Proclaiming you are one with God or simply God is not difficult as you may make it out to be. You do not do so by means of blind faith for that is unnecessary. You accept it as fact, a truth. You accept it with the same knowing as when someone asks you your name. It is what it is and who you know yourself to be.

You must be in constant awareness of your God self. If you live in constant awareness of your true self, it will be impossible for anyone to interfere, distract, or influence you from your harmonious, fruitful, and eternal life.

You are one with God and so you are your own Lord and Master. You must have no master or lord but God, the One Power. If you have a master outside your own, you are a slave. You are not a serf and you have been given dominion.

CHAPTER 6
Who You Are Not

"Everyone thinks of changing the world but no one thinks of changing himself."
~ Leo Tolstoy ~

♦

When you know who you are, you inherently know who you are not. If you know your name to be "John", then you will not respond when someone calls out "Peter". You know that is not you.

If you are born and raised in your original real home of love only – *Heaven*, then all that you would know is love. Only love would be in your consciousness. All else would be non-existent, unfamiliar, and unnatural. Your natural consciousness is love only. You are love – *God*. All else is not you.

There is no evil to overcome if you know no evil; evil does not exist. There is no stress to manage if there is no stress; stress does not exist. There is no fear to eliminate if you see and know love only; fear does not exist. There is nothing to do but be as you are – *God/love*.

God is good only (ie. love, joy, peace, compassion, et cetera). As such, it is easy to know and evident that if you are not-good (ie. fearful, angry, greedy, envious, et cetera), then you are not being who you are and you have forgotten who you are; if you see not-good in something or someone, then you are not being who you are; if you recognize not-good but do not judge it, you know that what you see is not God per se; if you experience not-good, you recognize that you forgot who you are.

Fear and all its derivatives (ie. anger, greed, envy, hate, worry, conflict, unhappiness, hastiness, et cetera), and all its physical illusions (ie. war, poverty, dis-ease, low self-worth, et cetera) explicitly demonstrate what is not God and who you are not. You do not identify with these things. You are none of this.

PART TWO
Claim Your Divinity

Your Natural Inheritance

CHAPTER 7
Parent & Child

"We are all asleep until we fall in love."
~ Leo Tolstoy ~

♦

This false world has endlessly made you forget who you are.

God created you but you did not create Him. He is your parent, your Father. You are His child.

God's greatest creation ostensibly is man. Likewise, the creation that gives a man and woman the most pride, joy, and fulfillment is their child, the ultimate expression of their love. You exist because you are important. This is true for your parents and their parents and so on because they are children of their parents and so on. You are loved by your parents because you exist. In like fashion, your existence proves that God loves you very much. You matter. Remember this *always*.

You as a child are the same. You love your parents because they exist; not because of what they do for you but because of who they are; because without them, you would not exist. In like fashion, you are to love God purely because of who He is for without Him, you would not exist. When you are unceasingly conscious that God is all in all, you see God in everything, including your fellow human being. And so, you radiate, impart, and show unconditional love to all for that is who you are and what you do.

Parents give birth to children, but children do not give birth to parents. They do, however, give birth to their children, and thus give birth as their parents do. Generations ensue. Children are extensions of their parents. They are forever connected to their parents. This is a bond that can never be broken. You are an extension of God. You are eternally connected to God.

God eternally sees and thinks you and all of His creations perfect. At no time does He see you as not being perfect. You as a parent see and think your child perfect when they are immediately born. However when you do not know who you are, you no longer see this everlasting perfection. Instead, you misperceive imperfections.

God loves you unconditionally. God does not judge so whatever you do (ie."good" or" evil"), you are always loved. God loves you in complete freedom to do as you will. God wants nothing more than His child to be happy; to do whatever brings him or her joy; and to be whoever he or she wishes to be. He allows His children the freedom of their own will. You as a true parent are the same. However when you do not know who you are, your love becomes conditional.

When you are unceasingly conscious that you are one with God and that God is all in all, you similarly do not judge anything, including your fellow human being. You only emanate, impart, and show unconditional love to all for that is who you are and what you do.

Parents teach their child what they know, yet the child still possesses free will as to what he or she chooses to learn and do. God teaches love and all things pure, noble, and good for that is what He is. God's children have free will to choose to follow God or not. If you are a parent and know not who you are, your child will not learn who they are either. Only when you personally expand your own self-awareness to know who you are will you then live truth. This is the truth that will set you free.

God's creative thought proceeds from Him to you, hence your own creative thought proceeds from you to your own creations. You continue the creative process through the creative abilities within you.

Parents desire to and willingly give everything to their children. In like fashion, God desires to and willingly gives everything to you. Parents typically leave all of their abundance to their children as an inheritance. The children need not work or pay for it but simply claim their heritage as it was rightly given to them. In like fashion, God gives His entire kingdom to you and all of His creations. You need not work or pay for it; you need only to accept your spiritual heritage. You claim your inheritance when you become like a child. This is to say, "Fear not, only believe."

Know this truth. All things of God are already yours and they are available to you. You have to merely accept and claim it. If you do not know who you are and this truth, you will unnecessarily struggle for the things you want and need. You must understand that the principal giver of all that you need is you and your ability to receive what you want. The way to receive your desires is simply to know what you want, know you are worthy of getting it, and know God has already provided you with it.

When you are unceasingly conscious of all the aforementioned, you should have and feel tremendous gratitude toward your parents, so express gratitude often to your parents; similarly, you should have and feel an overwhelming gratitude to God thus express constant gratitude to Him.

CHAPTER 8
Perfection

"By three methods we may learn wisdom. First, by reflection, which is noblest; second, by experience, which is bitterest; and third, by imitation, which is easiest."
~ Confucius ~

♦

God is perfect.

What does this mean? God is whole and complete. God is wholly love; wholly intelligence, wholly purity, wholly power, wholly light, wholly joy, wholly peace, wholly harmony, wholly happiness, wholly compassion, wholly kindness, wholly gratitude, wholly abundance, wholly calmness, wholly stillness, wholly inclusion, wholly expansion, wholly freedom, wholly non-judgment, wholly non-attachment, wholly non-resistance, wholly health, wholly youth, wholly beauty, wholly clarity, wholly knowledge, wholly wisdom, wholly good. God is wholly perfect good.

God is in and is a perfect good state always.

You are one with God. You are perfect.

God is all in all. Everyone is perfect. Everything is perfect. The world is perfect.

You may not see the perfection of yourself and the world around you because you do not fully know who you are as yet; because you misperceive perfection; because you misinterpret or misunderstand the meaning of the word perfection.

You perceive you are not perfect because you perceive you are not whole and complete as I described God in the earlier paragraph. You are not always kind, calm, and good; you are judgmental, attached, and resistant to things; you make "mistakes" (ie. miscalculated your shopping bill, painted the bedroom the wrong colour, scolded your child for something petty, et cetera). You degrade yourself to mean personal failure or unworthiness exemplifying to some degree your lack of self-love. Hence, you think and say, "I'm only human. I'm not perfect." You are wrong on both counts.

Let's say you want to make something such as a cake, a coffee table, or a romantic dinner. If it comes out exactly as you want, intend, or expect, then you say it is "perfect". If it does not come out exactly as you want, intend, or expect, then you say it is "not perfect". This is your current perception or interpretation of it. Perfection has no relevance to your expectations. In truth, it is "perfect" because the result is *exactly* as *you* created it, whether intentional or not intellectually. The floppy cake, the crooked table, and the disastrous dinner are also "perfect" because of what you did do based on your present mastery of its creation. The universe is a perfect mirror of you. So you see, you are "perfect".

As you progress to the truth – of who you are, *God*; of being the actual sole creator of your world, your life; of the intent of all things in your existence and the purpose of all action – you will see and understand the perfection of everything in your world. Like the cake, coffee table, and romantic dinner, you create everything exactly in your world according to who you are and what you do, whether you are conscious or unconscious of it. The perfection of your creation corresponds to the mastery of your innate power. You create consciously or unconsciously non-stop and the result is the physical which timely reflects your consciousness. It is your creativity in its current perfect form. You acknowledge and appreciate the moment-to-moment perfection.

Each circumstance, experience, and lesson is perfect for the growth, development, and evolution of yourself. Every piece is a perfect fit for a perfect puzzle that is the unity of all life – *Oneness*. There is no-thing that is a personal "imperfection" or "failure". As you embrace more of this perfection, along with the awareness of connectedness, you will be less resistant to apparent adversities and integrate more effortlessly all of the life around you. You see that all is to teach you to fulfill the highest expression of the divine presence within yourself. In so doing, you enhance the manifestation of good health, abundance, love, peace, joy, et cetera for yourself and inherently mankind.

The ability to see perfection in all things may be instantaneous or it may be a gradual learning experience. If you fully grasp who you are – *God*, you will have a true perception or perspective of perfection. If you do not, you will not. Conversely, if you have a true understanding of perfection, then it will help you to more firmly grasp who you are – *God* the creator. Be flexible with the dynamic of the two.

If you say you know who you are – *God* – and you say, "I AM rich, healthy, and good," but then walk down the street and say, "I see a poor beggar, a sick man, and an evil person," you are still not who you intellectually think you are and are not seeing correctly. You are only as perfect as you perceive or know others to be.

If you see a sick person, pray and hope he gets better, you judge wrongly. If instead you see a perfectly healthy man (ie. you envision him as he ought to be – vital and strong – not as he misperceived himself to be), you judge correctly. This principle applies to any negative attribute (ie. poor, bad, evil, et cetera) you misperceive. You recognize the presence and perfection of God and do not dwell on that which is seemingly not whole or perfect.

Change your conception of yourself and others and you will automatically change the world you live. When you appreciate the perfection of your circumstances, you then know to not try to change people. They are only messengers telling you who you are. Revalue yourself and they will confirm the change. By feeling the presence of God within you, you give glory of this indwelling presence to all. You reflect into the One Mind what you think and thus contribute to what others think.

God is all in all so It sees no evil or darkness anywhere for there is nothing but Itself. You deny yourself the truth of who you are. God waits for you and your consciousness to recognize It as yourself and your all-in-all. God waits for you to love yourself and your world. God waits for you to see, believe, and accept your own perfection.

CHAPTER 9
Oneness

"Give evil nothing to oppose and it will disappear by itself."
~ Lao Tzu ~

♦

God is all in all. So there is only one – *God*. God encompasses all things and is synonymous with the term, Oneness. From Oneness, all things are connected. In that sense, oneness and connectedness mean the same.

You have a synergetic relationship with the whole of every expression of God. You are in a continuous wondrous dance. You are like the one droplet of water with other droplets of water that make up the chain that the river is. This is to say that you are in God flow; God is flowing through you every moment. The river does not flow the way it does without you.

You are your own analogy. You are a planet. The physical planet you call your body is a perfect example of the totality of God. Within your living being, you are connected by your body parts that serve your whole being. You have given names to individual parts such as brain, head, eyes, ears, neck, lungs, heart, liver, kidneys, hands, arms, legs, red blood cells, and white blood cells.

Each body cell has intelligence, collaborates and serves every other cell. All individual cells naturally cooperate with each other for the higher good of your body. An organ, say your liver, within you would not intentionally harm the being, you, that contains it for that would mean its own death. Conversely, you would not intentionally hurt or cut off one of your own living parts, say your arm, because you are conscious though it is not the whole of you, that it is a part of you and that it serves you.

If you had a stomach ache causing you pain and suffering, you would not deem your stomach an evil enemy and instinctively retaliate to destroy it. You recognize that this is a symptom of internal distress not necessarily of its own accord but of which you played a significant part. You ate something disagreeable or poisonous; you are not nourishing your body with something it needs; you are not taking care of your physical vitality and so it is sensitive to anything that may unbalance it.

You accept responsibility for how you yourself contributed to what is causing the malfunction and the resulting pain that you experience. You act with compassion instead of in a combative manner. You take the necessary personal steps of a peaceful gesture to restore harmony because you see it as part of yourself and of the whole. The parts are not separate from you and they are not the whole of you but their summation is you – the one.

Likewise, humanity is God's body. Humanity composed of you and your fellow human beings, is simply one part of God amongst all other creations. You can consider water circulating God's system as you would your blood, continents as Its organs, trees as Its lungs, and all human beings as white blood cells circulating and serving Its entire Being. Each individual of humanity who remains unconscious is like a cancer cell within his or her own body that must evolve into a healthy one otherwise it contributes to destroying its own host and itself. Furthermore, a cancer cell will return to its healthy self when immersed in a healthy environment and surrounded by healthy cells. Similarly, one who is unaware of its true self will return to love in a world consisting of love inhabited with conscious loving souls.

War and violence, poverty, famine, et cetera are akin to the stomach ache. They are not evil circumstances by nature. You are to recognize them as symptoms of distress resulting from your possible contribution of how you are and what you are doing. The stomach ache is not the problem. You are the problem that caused your apparent problem. The food, medicine, or remedy you use to resolve the stomach ache is not the apparent solution. You are the real solution; your consciousness acknowledged your errant thinking to cause it and led you to use the good food, medicine, or remedy to heal the stomach.

You are only one individual part of many others. You are significant as all others. And all are significant as you are. You are one with God as all others are one with God too. When you are in constant awareness of who you are, God, Oneness, connectedness, you see God in all things.

The first thing that comes to your mind in your encounter with others is the similarities not the differences; the means to integrate, cooperate, and collaborate not compete; the friend not the enemy; the good not the evil; the light not the darkness; the perfection not the imperfection; the lesson and purpose not the challenge or accident; the learning opportunity not the adversity; the spirit not the physical body; the spirit not the personality; the God not the man.

When you focus mainly on a single part such as yourself, you overlook the whole, hence you separate. When you persistently identify with something, anything (ie. name, title, label, role, religion, group, class, category, type, job, country, object, person, idea, et cetera), you limit and separate yourself from that which you do not identify with. You unsuspectingly forget your wholeness. Your resulting habit is to see the differences of others. You lose sight of the God in all things. You lose the awareness of who you are – *God*.

CHAPTER 10
Spirit

*"There is not one path.
There is not even the right path.
There is only your path."*

♦

God is Spirit. You are spirit.

All desired changes in your outer reality begin with a change in your inner reality. An inner spirit of self-love and self-acceptance will radiate as true outer beauty.

You are the physical form of expression of God in Its likeness. This principle underlies all physical forms which are mere expressions from the contemplations of the originating spirit. Remember that all things must be spiritually conceived first to bring them forth into the physical. The physical is a mirror always giving you feedback on what is going on inside spiritually. With this understanding, know that when you experience a perceived negative physical challenge, you are prudent to not tackle it by physical means; you address the spiritual root first.

When you experience the likes of poverty, sickness, violence, et cetera, it confirms that you are not conscious – mentally thinking and being – of your true state: *God.* You developed the negative experience because of a poverty, sickness, violence, et cetera mindset, that not of God. The way to resolve the physical problem is to spiritually return to God – think and be of abundance, health, and all things good.

Know that though it is honourable to provide food, shelter, and help to those in need, charity is only a temporary means to soothe the wretchedness and it perpetuates the problem of lack, whether it displays itself as homelessness, poverty, famine, et cetera. The only way that such predicaments are eliminated permanently is by inspiring and teaching people about their divinity and their originating spirit. A man is better served when you teach him to spiritually fish rather than just give him a physical fish that only feeds him for one day.

CHAPTER 11
Responsibility

*"We have two lives and the second begins
when we realize we only have one."*
~ Confucius ~

♦

Responsibility is a portmanteau of the two words, response and ability. Responsibility means the ability to respond.

This false world has conditioned you to always look outside of yourself for anything and everything. Your current impulse now is to first look for that ability to respond elsewhere, not within yourself. When you have a problem, you look outside yourself for the solution. When you see a problem, you look to others to deal with the problem rather than thinking about how you can solve the problem. You shirk your self-responsibility – *your ability to respond*. You do this because you do not know about your own divinity and power; you have the luxury of blaming others; you favour laziness.

You are sick. You look to a doctor, a naturopath, a healer, et cetera. You are poor. You look to a government, a charity, a financial advisor, et cetera. You are depressed. You look to a doctor, a friend, a psychologist, et cetera. You look to others, give away your power, and naively accept their authority, word, and knowledge as absolute.

You are unhappy, angry, stressed, et cetera. You blame others or things outside of you for your circumstances. You look to an external means such as alcohol, drugs, or sex to elevate your state of mind. You are cruel, greedy, dishonest, et cetera. You blame the world for how you are because this is what you tell yourself you need to be to survive it.

There is war and violence, poverty, famine, dis-ease, homelessness, pollution, human trafficking, animal cruelty, planet destruction, et cetera. You look to others and a government entity to respond to it. You see these misfortunes as someone else's responsibility, not yours.

To be is to have. To have a problem shows you to be the problem.

If you truly reflect, you will notice that the more you evade your self-responsibility, the more your burdens become.

You are of your own free will however you appropriately decide to use thought. Your actions are your self-responsibility. If you use thought currency for your own selfish gain, then you are the one who must accept responsibility for its consequences. Undesirable negative consequences that result are there to make you weary and to teach you so that you eventually learn to turn back to God.

An individual's personal responsibility to choose correct over incorrect action for themselves is always their own. You can only erroneously believe and claim that you are "abdicating" personal responsibility for such choice to someone else. It can never actually be done in reality. The responsibility always belongs to you. You do not think for yourself. You alone allow your intellect and humanness to betray you. When you absolve yourself of full self-responsibility, you thoughtlessly obey any order from false authorities. It becomes more possible that you blindly obey immoral orders and then find convenient excuses for doing so. On a grand and extreme scale, you have genocide.

Once you know who you are and that you are the creator of your world, you willingly accept your responsibility to think for yourself; to change the bad experiences to good; to discern right and wrong action; to disobey immoral orders that cause you to harm others.

CHAPTER 12
Time

*"Only those who will risk going too far
can possibly find out how far they can go."*
~ T.S. Eliot ~

♦

Time is a created thing. *Now* is the only moment in "time". The past was a prior now and the future is a now yet to come. Time is a string of nows flowing together like the river of water molecules.

The more you align yourself with God, the more the concept of time becomes non-existent. This is to say, when you resist the truth, time develops; when you accept the truth, time dissolves.

Time is relative to the level of resistance you have of God. When you are experiencing joy in something you desire, you live in the present moment of now where you are not focused on a past memory or a future outcome. Time does not exist when you are immersed in reality from the joy of simply "being".

For example, if you spend time with someone whose company you do not enjoy, time slows down; you feel resistance to being stuck there in eternity. Conversely, if you spend time with someone you love, time seems to fly; you feel acceptance to being there in eternity.

When you see that every moment is perfect and has a specific purpose for you, you will not be focused on the past or the future. Instead, you will immerse and enjoy yourself more in the here and now of life.

When you know of your divinity and master your power (ie. have the right good thoughts, words, feelings, beliefs, faith, gratitude, et cetera), time begins to vanish because the truth of your new reality appears more quickly. The realization of answers to your questions, problems, and desires speeds into your consciousness. You see that in spirit, everything is real the moment it enters your consciousness.

PART THREE
Exercise Your Power

The Tools of the Trade

CHAPTER 13
Thought

*"Watch your thoughts; they become words.
Watch your words; they become actions.
Watch your actions; they become habits.
Watch your habits; they become character.
Watch your character; it becomes your destiny."
~ Lao Tzu ~*

♦

Thought is God in its most exalted form. Everything that is has come forth first from thought, which is the supreme intelligence called the mind of God.

Your mind and the mind of God are One.

Your mind is your internal instrument. Your body is the external instrument of you and your mind.

All things are first produced in the mind. The body is the outer reproduction of the inner thinking of your mind. Your body is the most creative and intimate expression of yourself. A right mind displays itself as a healthy body.

You are a creator and thought is the spiritual clay with which you sculpt your heart's desires. To think with your heart and mind is to create.

You must change your thoughts in order for your life to change. As your consciousness expands of who you truly are, your thoughts will change, become limitless, and you will move toward your new home and true reality – *Heaven*.

Your life in every moment is the sum of all your thoughts. Every physical manifestation and experience is an expression of your thoughts brought to life so that you may see your personal development and growth of your God self. Everything – the people, places, things, and events, whether you love them or hate them, fear them or desire them – comes from you.

You create the desired kingdom of God – *Heaven* – first through your loving thoughts (ie. thoughts of good, abundance, success, well-being, perfection, youth, et cetera). Good thought is akin to soap used to wash away the filth on your physical body – it purifies the filth in your spiritual mind. To say it another way, if you think good thoughts, you bear good fruit.

You must be vigilant and conscious of creating and sustaining your own thoughts. You may unsuspectingly allow your thoughts to be hijacked by others, through direct interaction (ie. person to person, family, friends, children, doctors, teachers, politicians, strangers, et cetera) or indirect means (ie. news, gossip, television, music, movies, social media, newspapers, magazines, et cetera).

To be is to have. To be in fear is to bear and have the fruit of fear.

Everything is invitation and consent. Poverty, dis-ease, war, human trafficking, et cetera can never enter your consciousness unless you invite, entertain, or believe in them. You are creating your creation and someone else is creating their creation. No one can intrude in your creation without your consent.

If someone is creating a reality for themselves that includes lack, misery, sickness, violence, et cetera, they cannot impose their reality upon you without your invitation and consent. They cannot draw you into their reality against your will. When you meet someone new or hear news or gossip, you begin to communicate your separate creations to each other and each is free to choose to accept or reject each and every part of that separate reality.

The world is filled with doomsters and naysayers persistently shouting every tragedy every moment. You are a subject of suggestion. Whatever suggestions you accept becomes part of you and your life. Each person who knows not who they are is hypnotized because his mind thinks what someone else tells it to think.

So many of the human race ignorantly think from its physical environment. You must not be dragged into the quagmire of the collective race consciousness. Though you perceive you are doing good by making others aware of world atrocities, you are likely contributing and precipitating the fear, negativity, and suggestions that are not of God. As a result, you breed and proliferate more fear into the world; you stray further away from who you are and become more of who you are not; you lead others away from the truth as you do yourself.

Many of this world have been seduced by fear for far too long. You must think, see, believe, and perceive only that you wish to experience and that is the perfection of God. This you will do when you know who you are – *God*. Then it is more valuable, beneficial, and constructive to reveal to others their divinity. You serve others better by teaching or reminding them who they are and how to rightly use their power. The world subsequently becomes the man and Heaven results.

CHAPTER 14
Words

"Nobody can bring you peace but yourself."
~ Ralph Waldo Emerson ~

♦

Words are power, wielded in love or fear.

God imagined the world, spoke the word into being and became that which It conceived. All creation rests on this principle.

You are one with God. You are power, truth, and law. Your word is power, truth, and law. Whatever you know or firmly believe to be true and speak it to be becomes so. This is your innate power.

When you have conviction with whatever it is you believe you are or have and express them into words, that is what you will be or have. Words have the power to raise and free you or to lower and limit you. As such, always be vigilant with the words you use.

Your world is your consciousness objectified. When you know who you are and when the truth of this fact dawns upon you, you will then know the mysticism of words which make flesh in the likeness of that which you are conscious of being.

God seeks expression through you, and how you express your desire through the words you speak with the innate knowing it is so, is how you bring forth the worldly expression into form. When you know you are God speaking your word, you will inevitably bring forth what is rightfully yours.

"I AM" is the nameless name of God. "I AM" is the word of power. When you say "I AM," you are proclaiming the presence of God within you. You are going to God directly. You are bringing forth the unconditioned formless consciousness of God into consciousness of form (ie. the image and likeness of your concept or ideal).

Whatever you affix to "I AM" and believe, you are in the now and become in the future now. Thus, if you say, "I AM rich" and believe you are rich, you are rich now and you become rich in the future now even if you are seemingly not so in the immediate now. Conversely if you say, "I AM poor" and believe you are poor, you are poor now and you become poor in the future now even if you are seemingly not so in the immediate now. Choose any word you desire or not desire (ie. strong/weak, happy/unhappy, unafraid/afraid, healthy/sick, et cetera) and that is who you are now and become in the future now even if you are seemingly not so in the immediate now. Continue to live in that spirit, that mental atmosphere and you will draw out that intelligence of God into being.

You begin to develop the fruit or nature of the thing you are feeling yourself to be as doubts vanish and you can feel "I AM this." Do not just believe IN God but believe God does everything for you as you ask. Note that to ask does not necessarily mean to do so in the form of a question. To state in words is to inherently ask. If for example you say, "I AM that," you are asking the nameless "I AM" to express "that".

Your word *is* law. You are the law unto yourself.

Words create separation.

Words belong to the world of form; they cannot truly express that which has no form. Words are but symbols of symbols. That is, the sun shines even without being called the sun, a tree grows even without being called a tree, and water nourishes even without being called water. That which is nameless is the unconditioned formless consciousness of God and that which is named has become an identified form of God consciousness.

Words are used to identify, describe, discern, or explain a form of expression of God. For instance, the word "rose" is used to distinguish it from a "tulip"; the word "cat" is used to distinguish it from a "dog"; the word "man" is used to distinguish it from a "woman"; the name "John" is used to distinguish it from "Peter"; et cetera.

God is all in all and without a diligent conscious recognition of this, the use of words inevitably obscures the connectedness between the various expressions of God, the oneness of all. You separate yourself from all of man, animal, thing, and all of nature. You no longer see yourself as part of everything and everything as a part of you, particularly your fellow man.

The challenge and irony of our intellectual world is to know that the moment you identify, describe, discern, or explain anything with words, you have actually lost its meaning and the One principle.

If you are not conscious of who you truly are and label yourself, for example, with the word "Catholic" and another a "Muslim," you separate from that person because you think and see yourself "different" rather than the same and as one – God; you may harm that person because you may now operate from fear rather than love – *God*.

If you are not conscious of who you are and label yourself, for example, with the word "citizen" and another "government," you separate from that entity because you think and see yourself "unequal" or "lower" rather than equal and as your own master – God; you may obey immoral orders because you now operate as a serf rather than a master of dominion – *God*.

If you are not conscious of who you are and label yourself, for example, with the word "man" and another "God," you separate from God because you think and see yourself "different" rather than the same and as one – God; you may be manipulated and submit to the creative power and energy from people outside of you instead of your own power – *God*.

Words create limits.

God is limitless. All conceptions are limitations of the limitless. That is, they are names of the nameless. "I AM" is the nameless unconditioned presence. When you use words and attach it to the "I AM" presence, you create a limit for God to express itself. That is, if you say "I am that," or "I have that," you are qualifying your consciousness with the "that" thing you are stating or seeking. When you complete the sentence, "I am that," you limit it because then you are not anything which is not "that". You are asking the Infinite Intelligence to express "that" which is finite otherwise it would remain formless.

God is unlimited and so you can limit the expression however you desire. You are one with God and so you have the power to attach yourself to any and all attributes of God: freedom, joy, abundance, health, success, wisdom, peace, perfection, et cetera.

CHAPTER 15
Belief & Faith

*"Faith is taking the first step even
when you don't see the whole staircase."*
~ Martin Luther King, Jr. ~

♦

Belief and faith are intertwined. Faith begins in belief. Both words describe the confident attitude in a person, thing or thing sought, idea, principle, or what-have-you and the undeniable expectancy of it. They are inseparable from you. Even when you do not believe in something, that in itself is a belief.

When you are a child, you inherently believe whatever your parents teach, tell, or say to you. When they tell you something – "you are beautiful," "do whatever you wish to do that makes you happy," "dinner is ready" – you accept their word. At no time do you doubt or question them. You have this innate belief and faith in them and that the statement is true. Your parents provide you everything even without your asking. Furthermore, they leave all that they have created in life to you as an inheritance.

You exhibit the same unwavering belief and faith when you visit a restaurant. After deciding what you want, you state your order to the waiter who tells you he will bring you your order. You never question thereafter whether your order will arrive. You have this innate belief and faith in him and that the statement is true. Everything is yours for the asking.

So it is with God. God is like your physical parent. He provides you with everything with or without your need to ask. He unconditionally loves you and wants to give you everything and in fact, He has and He does. And just like your waiter, He is always there and ready to give you anything you ask. Everything is your inheritance.

When you recognize, know, and accept God, you have steadfast belief and faith in God. You know that whatever you ask for, whatever you proclaim to be or have, you are or have.

If you ever doubt (ie. lack belief and faith), then that is a contradiction to God and yourself in that you do not really think, know, or accept you have everything. When you doubt receiving what you ask for, you are affirming that you do not have everything. As such, you do not receive it thereby confirming your true belief. This is the irony of belief and faith. God gives you evidence and proves to you what your true belief and faith is.

Do you see why faith makes you whole/God? It makes you whole/God because in reality you are whole/God already. Your faith simply acts to reveal that which already is. The works come automatically to the heart that believes.

Thoughts without faith create no forms. Only thoughts with faith have creative energy. It will be of no use to think about say, abundance if you do not have faith in abundance. If you do not have faith in abundance, then that means you have faith instead in poverty. Whatever you do not have faith in implicitly means you have faith in its counterpart. If you do not have faith in good then you have faith in the not-good.

A belief and faith in God is the foundation for faith in all things of God (ie. abundance, health, youth, perfection, et cetera). If you believe God, you have belief and faith that all things good are your natural state. The first step and only thing you really need to do to have faith in anything and applying it to yourself is to claim that it is the truth for that *is* what it is – *truth*. Mentally take the attitude that you are abundant, healthy, perfect, God, et cetera, and do not think, say, feel, or do anything which contradicts this attitude.

You can increase the power of faith without end. The power of faith is increased by having more faith because the expression of life results and correspondingly increases with it. This is to say, through faith that you already have what you desire, you give it first, and in turn, receive more of what you desire. Through this experience, your faith grows.

CHAPTER 16
Gratitude

"Life is simple but we insist on making it complicated."
~ Confucius ~

♦

Your atonement (ie. your oneness with God) and the whole process of abundance can be summed up in one word: *gratitude*.

Gratitude is the greatest aid to applying your faith and the most powerful form of prayer.

First, you recognize, believe, know, and accept that there is one intelligence – *God* – from which all things proceed. Second, you believe, know, and accept that God gives you everything you desire. Third, you relate yourself to it by a deep feeling of gratitude because you have the definite conviction in the reality of the unseen idea. And fourth, you receive the physical manifestation of that which was felt in the unseen or within yourself.

Expressing gratitude is easy to do because you already know how to be grateful. When someone gives you something, whether you ask for it or not, what do you typically say and how do you feel? You say, "Thank you," and you feel appreciative in your heart having received. How about the other way around? That is, when you give someone something (ie. you are showing your appreciation of them) and they explicitly say, "Thank you," what do you typically say and how do you feel? You say, "You're welcome," you feel appreciated, and you get a warm feeling in your heart. Furthermore, when the recipient shows appreciation, you have this natural tendency to want to give more to that person, don't you? They have returned the joy and appreciation you have given them so the sense of giving again remains with you. Conversely, if you give someone something and they neglect to thank you for it, would you be likely to give to them again?

You have that appreciative feeling when you receive something, more so especially when it is something you desire and ask for. When you fully recognize that God has given you everything and will give you anything you ask for, you will feel an overwhelming sense of gratitude. To express your gratitude, you simply say, "Thank you God."

When you feel grateful and voice your gratitude, you are affirming that everything is yours and that you have everything. As such, when you ask for something you desire and naturally express gratitude thereafter because you know you have it already, you hasten its arrival. Gratitude speeds the reception of things because it is an unequivocal assertion of your irrefutable belief and faith of having.

When you express your appreciation to God toward anything, no matter how little or insignificant it may seem, God has a tendency to give you more good things. Just as you like to see, hear, and feel gratefulness and appreciation for what you do for others, so does God. Be grateful even for the bad things or misfortunes in your life for they are there to teach you a lesson on what you need to change to be who you are. The more you appreciate, the more God gives you. When you know you already have, you will have more.

When you experience the results of gratitude, you will proclaim that it is only common sense. You will see that everything in life even your own existence is a gift to be thankful for. So give thanks to things you see that are and you have, and give thanks to those things that are not as though they are and they will appear.

Give thanks for the abundance, health, joy, peace, happiness, love, success, et cetera in your life now, you will have more in the future now even if you seemingly do not in the immediate now. The one whose mind knows that all prayers are answered and rejoices in joy with a grateful heart receives.

CHAPTER 17
Knowing

"Knowing others is wisdom; Knowing the self is enlightenment; Mastering others requires force; Mastering the self needs strength."
~ Lao Tzu ~

♦

To be is to have. Everything you experience in life comes through your own consciousness. Your state of consciousness represents what you think, feel, believe, and give consent to. Your state of consciousness is always made manifest. Nothing happens on the outside without first happening on the inside.

Before you can manifest a desire, a need, an anything, you must first possess your desire, your need, your anything in consciousness. You must have the feeling of possession inside.

God is all-knowing, hence the God Mind knows. When you do not know who you are, you think with a limited human mind because the human mind thinks not knowing that it intrinsically knows.

Knowing something is a great feeling. Knowing is so much better than not knowing, assuming, believing, and guessing. When you know something, you feel and experience the something throughout your body. When you know something and feel it, consciousness takes you there immediately where it is real.

When you know something, you experience certainty by an emotional feeling generally throughout your body. Knowing is the emotional ascertainment of the thing. If you know something good is coming, you feel a certain joy and satisfaction throughout your being. For example, when you know Christmas is coming, you feel joy and satisfaction knowing you are going to spend time with your family; when you know that your partner loves you, you feel joy and satisfaction knowing you are loved; when you know you bought a home, you feel joy and satisfaction knowing you are moving in soon.

When you newly discover who you are, you are unfamiliar as yet with your innate knowing. At the beginning of this new-found discovery, you will have to intellectually process this knowing. This means that you need to qualify your mind with the consciousness or feeling of having or being that thing you desire. You mentally reject completely any arguments against it. You do this until you reach a conviction in your consciousness whereby the problem no longer annoys or worries you because you are in possession of it. When you maintain this mental poise, you will be or have the thing you desire.

As you assimilate the true nature of being who you are, you will no longer need to intellectualize the process. You will have accepted the truth of who you are, that you have been provided everything, and that all is for your taking. The knowing feeling (of being or having) will naturally follow when your consciousness is filled with the concept you desire. Words, thoughts, beliefs, faith, and gratitude all meld into knowing which eventually becomes being. They are the baking ingredients and recipe to make the cake that is you.

Recognize that a desire is nothing more than the thought of fulfillment seen through an object, entity, or experience. So once you think of a thing you desire, you should instantly have a knowing feeling and gratitude because you know that it is fulfilled.

Always affirm your God-knowing and hold the thought that you know even in midst of your prior habit of uncertainty. Do not judge by appearances. The Divine Mind will reveal itself to you through your intuition when you are wholly aligned with It.

Knowing is a feeling. Knowing is receiving.

CHAPTER 18
Blessing

"Your desire to change must be greater than your desire to stay the same."

♦

To bless means to wish, confer, endow, favour, magnify, glorify, praise, or exalt all things divine (ie. abundance, prosperity, health, happiness, joy, peace, love, et cetera) upon a person, thing, place, event, situation, or experience. Similarly, to be blessed means to have divine things.

Bless anything and it will bless you. Bless the good and more good will come upon you. Bless the seemingly not-good (ie. enemies, negative persons or circumstances, et cetera) and your personal blessing turns them into good for you.

When you are consciously aware of being blessed and of your blessings, you inevitably become grateful for them. As indicated in the section of gratitude, when you are grateful, you attract more blessings into your life. When you give thanks, you inherently bless it. Bless the little and the little becomes a lot. Blessing and expressing gratitude are essentially twin sisters.

When you are conscious to bless negative people, circumstances, events, and experiences, it demonstrates that you are one with God because you are imparting good thoughts, words, and energy despite the apparent negativity. You are exhibiting your love.

Just as with gratitude, bless all in your life no matter how little or insignificant it seems. Bless your body, home, car, friends, family, enemies, rude people, adversities, trees, earth, sun, water, air, et cetera because they are all God for your use and learning.

PART FOUR
Get There

Directions

CHAPTER 19
I AM

"When I let go of what I am, I become what I might be."
~ Lao Tzu ~

♦

To begin, say and live with the feeling, "*I AM one with God,*" all day long. Feel your connection to God, this unseen Spirit and Infinite Intelligence, as you do with your own physical mother or father. Keep repeating this until you satisfactorily feel the deep connection.

Now, say and live with the feeling, "*I AM God,*" all day long. Feel you are this, continue to live in that mental atmosphere, and you will draw out the God (wisdom, power, and intelligence) within you. Your whole world will be transformed by that inner light shining in your mind.

Once you are comfortable that you have made the assimilation, shorten your words to "*I AM*". By this, you are returning to the original name of God that is pure, absolute, unexpressed, and unlimited power. You are proclaiming the power and presence of God within you. Say it over and over lovingly, earnestly, expectantly with the knowing until you have lost all consciousness of the world and know yourself just as being. Do not try to define what it means nor analyze your feelings but just say it and it will begin to reveal itself to you. Soon you will find your whole being filled with a sense of power that you never had before – a power to overcome, a power to accomplish, a power to do all things.

When you understand the simplicity of the "I AM" declaration, you understand your true being. Having accomplished this, whenever you so desire, attach "that" desire you wish to define yourself along with the knowing feeling (ie. "I AM that") and "that" will be expressed in your world. You will be the recipient of all its goodness and love.

The "I AM" is the true self, *the God within*. Always speak upwardly toward the good and true. Never speak downwardly (ie. "I am sick," "I am poor," "I am afraid," "I am stupid," et cetera) for these are false claims. God cannot be these false statements because It is all-power, all-good, and all-life.

You *are* all. You *have* all. Simply *know* it and nothing other.

Once you definitively know who you are and that you alone are responsible for creating all in your life, you will be vigilant with your words, thoughts, feelings, and actions. This collective world can only change one person at a time and the change can only be made by the individual themself. You must be the change you want to see in yourself and in the world.

When you wholly know who you are (*"I AM"*), you no longer need to try or practice eliminating fear for it does not exist in your consciousness. Your natural state of love is the only thing that exists. You have reached your destination – *Heaven*.

CHAPTER 20
Balance

"It does not matter how slowly you go as long as you do not stop."
~ Confucius ~

♦

Perfect balance and harmony is a neutral state of mind where you feel clarity, contentment, and well-being. There is only a simple sense of peace. You do not need any condition outside of you to achieve this balanced state. When you are in balance, it means you are in the moment; you are not thinking about the past or future; you are not looking at things right or wrong; you are not seeing yourself as "better than" or "less than"; you are in complete acceptance of yourself and the world around you.

Do the following to attain and remain in balance.
- Know that you are loved, you are important, and you matter.
- Exercise constant gratitude for your life (ie. existence).
- Accept you have (been given) everything.
- Accept you are worthy and worthy of everything.
- Accept there is a purpose for what is happening to you and around you.
- Accept where you are in life in relation to everything else in existence.
- Develop complete love and understanding for yourself, knowing that in every moment, you are perfect and all else is perfect around you.
- Gain understanding and compassion despite experiencing any form of hurt, pain, or suffering.
- Become aware that all things are possible; there are endless possibilities and opportunities.
- Do not become attached to any identity while enjoying the experience of it.
- Remain faithful to the outcome of anything desired.

CHAPTER 21
Creation

"If you want to awaken all of humanity, then awaken all of yourself. If you want to eliminate the suffering in the world, then eliminate all that is dark and negative in yourself. Truly, the greatest gift you have to give is that of your own self-transformation."
~ Lao Tzu ~

♦

Everything reproduces after its own kind.

Your mind is a creator-yes-now machine. Your input thoughts determine the physical output which reflects in kind, the summation of what it was given. You are responsible for both your own positive and negative experiences.

You reap what you sow. You receive what you give. That is, if you think good thoughts, you bear good fruit; if you think bad thoughts, you bear bad fruit.

For practical purposes, you may find it helpful to think of all dichotomies (ie. good/evil, peace/conflict, higher-self/lower-self, et cetera) akin to the hot and cold temperature of a shower faucet. They are simply two attributes of one. As you journey to your true self – *God*, your mind (consciousness) is the shower faucet you use to adjust between the two aspects to attain the ultimate balance you continually seek – that sense of clarity, peace, and well-being. To be one with God is to achieve balance – *Heaven*.

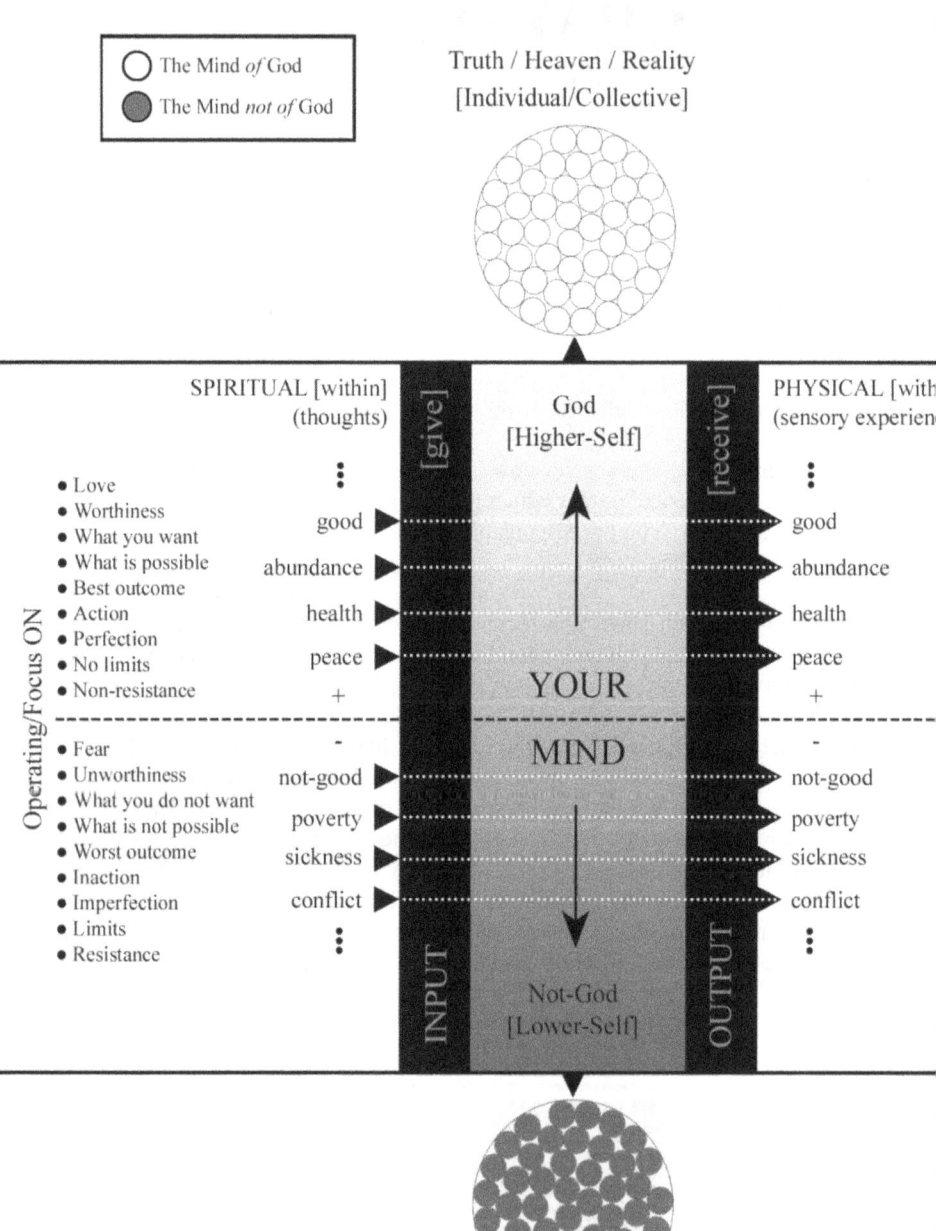

CHAPTER 22
Acceptance

"Be the change you want to see in the world."
~ Mahatma Gandhi ~

♦

Your destination is Heaven. Move beyond recognizing, believing, and knowing. See what a change it makes for you. Simply accept the truth.
- God LOVES you.
- You MATTER.
- You are spirit.
- You and God are one.
- You are just one unique individual physical expression of God.
- You are your own Redeemer and your own Saviour.
- You are eternal and infinite.
- You are absolute, whole, complete, and perfect.
- You are invincible.
- You have power.
- You have the capabilities of God.
- You have been given everything; whatever you need and want is always provided.
- You are always safe.
- You are the creator of all your world's creations.
- All the above is true for every man and woman.

Because you are conscious of the aforementioned things in every moment always, be the change you want to see in the world.
- You live consciously.
- You think and act consciously thereby create consciously.
- You operate from love only and focus on what you want.
- You see (the good of) God in yourself, everyone, and everything.
- You give your love freely, unconditionally, and endlessly.
- You keep your thoughts centred always on God who is perfect.

- You are and feel constantly grateful to God; and you express your gratitude always.
- You know you are your own master.
- You are the master of your mind and consciousness.
- You are the master of your physical urges and temptations, your emotions and mental attitude, and your outer surroundings (ie. people, things, environment, et cetera), not the other way around.
- You are non-judgmental, non-attached, and non-resistant.
- You have inner self-love, self-acceptance, self-confidence, self-belief, self-worth, et cetera.
- You are in a state of joy, peace, and content.
- You are the love, joy, and peace.
- You know your word is power, truth, and law.
- You live in the present moment of now.
- You think and act as God, and thereby experience all things God that is good.
- You neither operate from fear nor focus on what you do not want.
- You no longer fear anything in life but instead you love everything in life.
- You are no longer influenced or upset by negative thoughts, suggestions, and actions of others.
- You never allow people who do not know who they are to distract you from being who you are.
- You lose sight of personality, of divisions and differences, and are always conscious of your oneness with everyone and with God. You see God in everything.

CHAPTER 23
Love

*"Just as one candle can light another and
can light thousands of other candles,
so one heart illuminates another heart and
can illuminate thousands of hearts."*
~ Leo Tolstoy ~

♦

You have a greater impact on people by who you are rather than by what you have or what you do.

When you operate on love, you focus on what you desire without any attachment to them. The answers come into your reality based on who you are because God is anxious to give it to you as you are to get it. Your role is to know you are worthy, see and claim it. When you love yourself, you love God; when you love God, you love not only yourself, but everyone and everything.

There is an eternal state of realities coinciding with yours. Each person, place, or thing is God expressing the perfection of matching intents, and providing a learning opportunity of love for all involved. God is always working with elegant precision and unfaltering intelligence.

The most effective way to help in the healing of another human being is to be the God that you inherently are. When you are, you come from a place of understanding, compassion, acceptance, and unconditional love. This is because you are the love that you are – *God*. When you are not at this level of understanding and being (ie. you judge, criticize, condemn, resist an afflicted individual's behaviour, et cetera), you affirm a person's lack of self-worth. The more you know God loves and accepts you, the more you can offer this love and acceptance to yourself and others. You let your own light shine so that you unconsciously give others permission to do the same. When they see and experience the God in you, they will begin to see it in themselves. They will come closer to knowing God is within them too.

We are all One Mind. Each person who knows of their divinity and accepts it, contributes to helping those unaware become aware. *You are now one such person.* The greatest treasures in heaven are you and the people you help to get there. Raise yourself and you will raise others.

Epilogue

*"Blessed is the lion which a man eats so that
the lion becomes the man. But cursed is the man
whom a lion eats so that the man becomes the lion."*
~ Gospel of Thomas ~

♦

If you reflect on your present conditions, you will recognize that if you lack something or have not accomplished something you desire, it is because you are operating and focused on hidden fears; lack of self-worthiness; what you do not want; what is not possible; the worst outcome; inaction; judgment; attachment; resistance. You are afraid, pessimistic, and unenthusiastic of being "lesser" than where you are. This is *not* the God within you who is eternal and infinite wanting to expand yourself.

If you reflect on your present conditions, you will recognize that if you have something or have accomplished something you desire. it is because you are operating and focused on love; self-worthiness; what you do want; what is possible; the best outcome; action; non-judgment; non-attachment; non-resistance. You are bold, optimistic, and enthusiastic of being "more" than where you are. This is the God within you who is eternal and infinite wanting to expand yourself.

Knowing the truth of who you are is pivotal and fundamental to everything in your world – the apparent problems and the solutions. You must know of your divinity, your power, and how to rightly use this power. When you do not know who you are and of your power, you allow the external world to affect how you think, act, and be rather than you affecting the world by the energy you transmit; everything then works backwards; the world flips itself upside down.

The world can have an enormous impact on you when you know not who you are. Let's look at how you allow the world and others impact you and your world when you are unaware of your divinity.

The world is currently consumed with countless atrocities (ie. wars, poverty, dis-ease, human trafficking, pedophilia, massacres, genocide, oppression, pollution, planet destruction, disasters, famine, crimes, suicides, animal cruelty and slaughter, et cetera) that capture your attention. As these enter your reality, your reaction (based on your power to choose) produces a response that works its way back to the tragedies you see.

Your current habit could be to feel frustration, anger, depression, sadness, et cetera). Your energy shifts to a negative polarity. Your negative state of mind strengthens the negative energy of the world thereby sustaining all such unwanted realities. Your power to manifest positive change is suppressed because you are now engaged in stories that put and keep you in a negative state of mind.

There are constant news and propaganda of endless atrocities and calamities in the world. When you disseminate information about such under the guise of raising awareness, perceiving it as a good way to end them, you are conceivably perpetuating them. You are feeding the thoughts to more unaware people thereby potentially breeding more fear and negativity into the world and naively leading others further away from truth. As such, you help sustain this false world.

For all these senseless situations, you need to first accept what already is. Acceptance does not mean you condone it. It means you rise above and understand it for why it is occurring. You move beyond a negative reaction to a state of mind that begins to change it.

Remember the principle that all physical forms are mere expressions from the contemplations of an originating spirit; all things must be spiritually conceived first to bring them forth into the physical; the physical is a mirror always giving you feedback on what is going on inside spiritually.

Actions to help "fix" world problems like circulating information to raise awareness, creating private member associations, teaching others how to get "off the grid", and so on, though valuable are not necessarily permanent long-term solutions. These "solutions" do not effectively address the spiritual root of the problem. They are tackling physical circumstances through physical means. The desired change must be brought about spiritually as that is its origin.

So, will you be in turmoil, continue to respond negatively, and be consumed by the world or will you be at peace, respond positively, and consume the world by accepting who you are and using your power?

You are a creator. Everything that results or does not result, good or bad, is because of you. The moment you realize who you are – *God* – and that you create it all, you will realize that you can change it all.

You are one with God. You are love. You accept this for yourself and you emanate this. You no longer blindly follow those unaware. You serve someone better when *you* inspire him to spiritually know he *is* the solution rather than just hand him the illusion of a physical solution that only gets him by for one more day.

KNOW WHO *YOU* ARE.

ACCEPT WHO *YOU* ARE.

BE WHO *YOU* ARE.

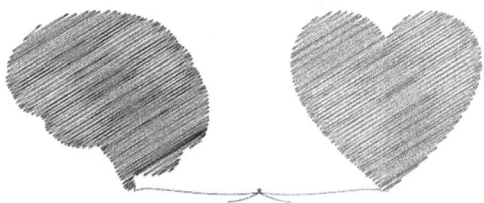

*The road to Heaven is in your mind.
The directions to get there are in your heart.*

www.ingramcontent.com/pod-product-compliance
Lightning Source LLC
Chambersburg PA
CBHW070655050426
42451CB00008B/364